Conrad Hilton Quotes

By Mr. Gerald Myers

Disclaimer:

The information in this book is based on the author's knowledge, experience and opinions. The methods described in this book are not intended to be a definitive set of instructions. You may discover other methods and materials to accomplish the same end result. Your results may differ.

There are no representations or warranties, express or implied, about the completeness, accuracy, or reliability of the information, products, services, or related materials contained in this book. The information is provided "as is," to be used at your own risk. The author assumes no liability for actions that you perform and any resulting damage to yourself, others, or property.

This book is not intended to give legal or financial advice and is sold with the understanding that the author is not engaged in rendering legal, accounting or other professional services or advice. If legal or financial advice or other expert assistance is required, the services of a competent professional should be sought to ensure you fully understand your obligations and risks.

This book includes information regarding the products and services of third parties. We do not assume responsibility for any third party materials or opinions. Use of mentioned third party materials does not guarantee your results will mirror those mentioned in the book.

All trademarks appearing in this book are the property of their respective owners.

Contents:

Quotations:

Success seems to be connected with action. Successful men keep moving. They make mistakes, but they don't quit. ~ Conrad Hilton.

To achieve big things you have to have big dreams. ~ Conrad Hilton.

To achieve big things you have to have big dreams. ~ Conrad Hilton.

No matter how late we worked into the night, I started the day on my knees. ~ Conrad Hilton.

If you want the dull, tame life, if you have no compelling dreams or head for achievement, stay on the ground, away from big business. ~ Conrad Hilton.

Enthusiasm is a vital element toward the individual success of every man or woman. ~ Conrad Hilton.

To accomplish big things, I am convinced you must first dream big dreams. ~ Conrad Hilton.

Success is never final; failure is never fatal. ~ Conrad Hilton.

I can think of no greater God-given responsibility we have than that of extending a helping hand to our fellow man. ~ Conrad Hilton.

To some degree, you control your life by controlling your time. ~ Conrad Hilton.

My mother had one answer, one cure, for everything. Prayer! ~ Conrad Hilton.

We earned every penny we got. ~ Conrad Hilton.

It always started with a dream. ~ Conrad Hilton.

To be haunted by past failures or satisfied with past successes is to arrest forward motion. ~ Conrad Hilton.

There's a vastness here and I believe that the people who are born here breathe that vastness into their soul. They dream big dreams and think big thoughts, because there is nothing to hem them in. ~ Conrad Hilton.

Remember to tuck the shower curtain inside the bathtub. ~ Conrad Hilton.

Charity is a supreme virtue, and the great channel through which the mercy of God is passed onto mankind. ~ Conrad Hilton.

There is a natural law, a Divine law, that obliges you and me to relieve the suffering, the distressed and the destitute. ~ Conrad Hilton.

If you climb Mount Everest, no matter how carefully you plan, anything can happen. Your ice axe slips, your oxygen gives out. A concealed crevasse swallows you up. Well, that's about the way it was building my first Hilton Hotel. ~ Conrad Hilton.

Dig for gold. It means utilization of every possible foot of space for the production of maximum income. ~ Conrad Hilton.

Additional Books by Gerald Myers, Which You Can Find on Amazon.com:

1. 50 Sudoku Puzzles

2. 550 Conversation Starters and Fascinating Facts

3. A Bucket List That Will Turn Lambs into Lions

4. A Cross Section of Tattoo Specimens

5. Aesop's Quotations

6. Air Force Quotations

7. Air Guns' Evolution, Safety, and New Jersey's Applicable Laws

8. Alan Watts' Quotes and Sayings

9. Albert Einstein: The Things You Should Know

10. American Holidays and Important Dates to Remember

11. An Anthology of Ephemeral Stories

Printed in Great Britain
by Amazon

47293154R00020